THE FUTURE

OF

BOOK
PUBLISHING

THE FUTURE
OF
BOOK
PUBLISHING

JOEL STAFFORD

ISBN-13: 979-8-6664-7037-4

Website:
www.Joelbooks.com

Facebook: facebook.com/joelsbooks
Instagram: instagram.com/joelsbooks

First edition: August 2020

TABLE OF CONTENTS

NEW WAYS OF PROTECTING READERS

In 2020, at the start of the pandemic (March-May), we experienced a fascinating phenomenon. A lot of books appeared in coronavirus topic, simply because of its popularity. "COVID-19" and "coronavirus" became one of the most searched keywords not only on Google but also on Amazon.

In the first wave "COVID-19 news" style books appeared on Amazon. I would say up to 20-30 every week, but maybe I underestimate the figures. The primary issue with these books was that they were mainly plagiarized and copy-pasted from the major news sites, and they lacked any empirical evidence or background research. If fake news appears on a website, it could easily become part of these "COVID-19 news" books. Which is an issue for us, readers. People aren't in the position to check the truth of any content they buy in a book. Planarization was just the tip of the iceberg.

Amazon decided to simply remove these books (all of them) from his marketplace in March and it continued this policy during the summer. This was a drastic step from the e-commerce giant, but from a practical point of view, I would agree with their decision. There was no cost-effective process or technology to validate the content of these books. And the risk was too high on the other side: letting potentially misleading information to the public in the form of a **book**.

We realized — but it isn't new at all — that the quality check function of the publishers was gone. In the past, publishers simply didn't accept manuscripts that hold non-verified major information or plagiarism, but this changed with the emergence of pre-paid publishers and self-publishing.

Now in 2020, suddenly became the task of marketplaces to protect their readers from fake news.

In the world of SEO, we use a service called Copyscape on daily basis. This plagiarism detecting tool finds web pages where the same sentences appear, which means someone copy-pasted the content. This type of behaviour infringes the copyright of the original content owner. The tool helped millions of people to validate the uniqueness of any article, and it became an industry standard.

In case of books we don't have any similar tools, which could compare two books or identify any text that matches in two books. This kind of tool — let's call it Global Content Uniqueness Overseer — will be essential in case of book marketplace operators. Both marketplace owners (like Amazon, Barnes & Noble, etc.) and readers need to know whether a book holds unique content or plagiarised.

Protecting readers from specific topics

I'm not here to judge whether controlling or restricting any type of fiction or non-fiction topic is good or bad for online book marketplaces. In the past traditional bookstores reserved the right not putting out anything to their shelves, the same principle could be valid for big online book marketplaces in 2020. Will it be a new type of censorship?

At the beginning of June, a former New York Times reporter published a short book on Amazon, which was immediately removed from the marketplace. After the case, Elon Musk tweeted to Jeff Bezos, that it is "This is insane". The events clearly doesn't meet Musk's standards. After several hours Amazon put back the 22 pages short book of the author, and now one of the most popular books in that niche, thanks to Musk's tweet.

This whole situation is clearly the battle of values. Amazon would like to control somehow their book's quality which could damage their reputation seriously after the pandemic but knows they were influenced directly because of one title, which isn't fair to those who published a quality book (and I'm not talking about the plagiarised books) and removed from the store after several weeks.

The future could be exciting in this manner. What if people may hold their potential to restrict a particular type of book categories for themselves. For example, if they don't want to see books about "COVID-19 News" or simply low-quality books based on cover or description. It is clear that the importance of personal AI assistants will emerge. These AI agents will protect our preferences. They will have much more sophisticated data protection abilities than the cloud-based solutions have today (Google Now, Apple's Siri or Amazon's Alexa). Their ultimate role would be to take away the filtering part from publishers and marketplaces.

THE RISE OF AUDIOBOOKS

Audiobooks have a rich history, they appeared first in 1932, but in reality, they received attention when the MP3 technology appeared in 1992, which enabled users to carry more books "in their pocket". Usability still was an issue for years, even when everybody understood that sound industry is ahead of significant changes, just think about the appearance of iPods in 2001.

Amazon realized the potential in audiobook and put a lot of effort to make it happen. The company group understood that it is a three-element game:

1. **Marketplace** - People need a marketplace where there is a big amount of content, so they acquired **Audible** in 2008 (launched in 1995)
2. **Production** - Authors need easy access for audiobook creation, so Amazon launched its ACX platform in 2011
3. **Marketing** - The third and not an obvious point was the rise of the popularity of audiobooks. Amazon spent a lot of marketing dollars on their platforms to advertise their new Audible brand

Well, the formula seems to be simple, but it is a challenging game, and it was a big investment also on

Amazon's side. Readers are not early adopters, and it was clear after the appearance of ebooks, that the market will have a long development path, and it won't be an instant success. It wasn't. Readers need to get used to new technologies like Kindle Readers (Paperwhite, Oasis, etc.) smartphones and tablets. Then they have to get enough courage to break with their old book reading habit and try reading a book on these electronic devices.

The same path awaited for audiobooks. Thanks to the popularity of smartphones, the devices were there in our pocket, but listening to a book was a brand new experience for most of us.

Fast forward, in Dec. 2019 Deloitte predicted a 25% growth in the audiobook market for 2020, reaching the high $3.5 billion. That's huge growth. Of course, life may have another opinion with the COVID-19 crisis, but one thing we experienced during the last months (March-May 2020) that global sales numbers for non-popular (mostly self-published) book titles has a roughly 5%-20% drop, and the big winners were the top-rated book titles. Even the effectiveness of different advertising forms worked significantly worse.

Since we mainly work with self-published titles, we struggled in the last months. According to McKinsey research, the customer behaviour changed thanks to the pandemic significantly. The households' income dropped in these months, and a lot of people sadly lost their job. An average consumer in the US reported decreasing their spending by 25% according to the study, which may have a direct effect on the upcoming months. We know that optimism-income and spending behaviour has a direct correlation. At the end of the day, a drop in sales numbers in the book market will appear sooner or later.

The catch is that we couldn't experience this with audiobooks and Audible. There wasn't a dropped, or even if it was it limited the development potential of the market in the last months. Even without significant marketing, we could experience decent sales numbers on Audible.

This is why we suggest to our authors to release their book on Audible quicker than the paperback. From a marketing point of view, it is the best investment that an author could make.

Now we need to put this into perspective. Let's see how big the different markets are at the moment (Deloitte Insights for 2020):

- Esports ($1.3 billion)
- **Audiobooks** ($3.5 billion)
- Movies ($45 billion)

- Subscription video on demand ($60 billion)
- Newspapers ($135 billion)
- **Books** ($145 billion)
- Video games ($160 billion)

How these markets and their share will change in the following 10 years:

- Esports ($3-4 billion)
- **Audiobooks** ($15-30 billion) **300%-750% increase**
- Movies ($60 billion)
- Subscription video on demand ($100 billion)
- Newspapers ($100 billion)
- **Books** ($100-110 billion) **25% decrease**
- Video games ($240 billion)

Why are we saying that traditional book formats will generate lower sales in the upcoming years than audiobook or movie formats?

Entertaining products have their evolution, and we already know this path:

1. Written entertainment (books)
2. Sound entertainment (audiobooks)
3. Audio-visual entertainment (audio-visual books)
4. Motion picture entertainment (movies)

People prefer more complex sensory experiences, over they should generate with their own imagination, which means audiobook isn't the final stage.

One question whether this means, that the old fashioned forms of entertainment will disappear? The answer is no. Their popularity will shrink, but I'm sure they won't disappear. They might change and evolve. What if we could ask a future Harry Potter book to place us in the Hogwarts? It is sci-fi at the moment but could be reality tomorrow.

Now we get a quick insight into the relevance of audiobooks, and why it is considered the success of tomorrow's entertainment business. As a writer, we should also acknowledge the importance of that platform, and we should adapt. We know that audiobook market works and there are some big players there like:

- Audible.com
- Audiobooks.com
- Librivox.org – Public domain books
- Google Play (Audiobooks section)
- Kobo.com (Audiobooks section)

In terms of market share Audible certainly has a significant advantage, the site ranked at 926th on Alexa while Audiobooks.com was only 29,969[th] position.

THE "NETFLIX EFFECT"

As you may already figure out, this book isn't just about the near future. We are focusing here on the big picture of what could happen in the next 10-20 years with the book publishing ecosystem.

It is said that Netflix is a game-changer in movie distribution and how people are consuming motion pictures. But when we say "Netflix effect," we think of something else in case of the book industry.

In the US there are around 1,100-1,200 new TV shows (including series and movies) in a year. In 2019, Netflix created 371 TV shows which were 50% more than in 2018 according to Variety. Now, as we see the numbers in perspective, we need to admit Netflix became a game-changer not only the consumer market but also on the production side.

But what are the advantages that make the company so successful:

- **Unified brand** – Which means they need to spend less money on marketing, because of the subscription model and customers will be more loyal to the platform in the long term

- **Alternative revenue model** – Subscription model instead of watching annoying traditional commercials. Netflix understood that people hate commercials which destroy the entertaining factor of watching a longer movie or a TV episode
- **Trying out new content** – Netflix can take more risks when deciding to put a story into production. Netflix Originals include a lot of not traditional titles. Netflix is risking to air new, uncommon, sometimes foreign titles like the German series "Dark" was in 2017.
- **Mass production of content** – And finally we arrived at the most important point. Netflix understood that its new revenue model wouldn't work without enough unique content, so they put considerable effort into the production part. Netflix isn't thinking in single titles but whole product lines and stories.

Netflix effect isn't just about putting personalized content in front of subscribers. Still, also, **they innovated the management of mass content creation**, and this would be a critical factor in the future.

At the university, I learned that there are two kinds of innovations:

1. Innovating a new product, something we have never seen before
2. **Innovating a process**, when the final product will be in the same quality, but the process is completely new

Netflix did the second. Of course, they have a lot of new content, but who doesn't in the competitive TV industry? **They developed the process on how to mass-produce a lot of TV shows and movies.**

Let me tell you the story of *floating glass*.

The glass used for windows wasn't as cheap as it is today, as a matter of fact, glass was really expensive, especially if you wanted bigger surfaces.

Between 1953 and 1957 Pilkington Brothers developed a process where they created huge glass surfaces using molten tin. The attributes of the produced glass were better than the traditional production process, but the best part was the production became much cheaper. The Pilkington process enabled architects to revolutionize the look of the skyscraper.

Well, Netflix does something very similar to the filming industry. The company wants to push down the prices while expecting the same quality of end products in case of original shows. And it works, especially in case of small budget productions. Netflix produced a lot of quality TV shows. While there are the big titles like Game of Thrones was several years ago, where HBO paid around $15 million for only one episode. The tendency is clear; quality is reachable with even small production teams. Now we can produce a TV episode from $75,000-200,000 in the US.

Motion picture and making good movies isn't the privilege of Hollywood in 2020. A lot of new players stepped into the game in the last 10 years. What we see is the shrink of post-production costs, talented actors everywhere and accessible motion effects and visuals.

This whole new world will end up to the rise of the importance of the story itself. Between 1990 and 2015 we saw that Hollywood produced a lot of zero story movies, usually comedy films and action movie remakes, where they expected the success thanks for the actors or the visuals. **These years passed**; hence Hollywood still didn't recognize that, but Netflix did. Netflix tries to break the tradition of no-brain films. People love stories which make them think. But Netflix, HBO and Disney aren't so naive to pick random stories; they try to target the best. Best from the past and best from the present and **these stories are in the form of books now.**

Amazon's bookstore became the biggest library of the motion picture industry. **They check the success books since the book market could validate the strength of a story.** By the time I'm writing these lines, Ernest Cline's new novel "Ready Player Two" just appeared in the Amazon store for pre-sale. I would bet that the managers of Warner Bros. Pictures — who produced the movie Ready Player One — will be watching the numbers of the sales in the upcoming months. They need to know whether it is worth to produce a sequel.

What we expect in the forthcoming years that the value of the good stories will raise. They are easily accessible at the moment, but searching for a new quality, and unique story is an extremely hard task. There have been a lot of books released per year, but they're only a couple of really good stories between them.

Thanks to the big publishers who are really good at marketing, their new titles will become even a success when their story isn't strong at all, but this is book business after all. The numbers we see on Amazon aren't full proof, once an expert said that strong stories emerge only in every five years.

TWITCH AND LIVE STREAMING

Twitch live streaming platform appeared in 2012, and it was sub-brand of Justin.tv. Now the main brand only exists in Wikipedia, but Twitch started something new: the age of live entertainment content. Was that something new? Not at all. The entertaining adult website Livejasmin was the first who invented this live experience in 2002, ten years before Twitch! But Twitch was the first who could implement this approach to wider audiences with gaming content.

Why is this relevant? How does this connect to book publishing?

In the last chapter, I pointed out that stories and content will represent the main value in the future.

Movies and motion picture itself are just one form of entertaining products. We spoke about audiobooks in the first chapter, and live content is a new kind of entertainment for younger generations. The genre isn't new, since live talk shows and stand up comedies are very similar, but there is one key difference between those traditional shows and live streaming. Streamers on Twitch aren't professionals. They don't have any pre-written script, not even a plan for the live, but **people —**

Generation Y, Z and Alpha — **love them**. Michael Grzesiek, or as the gamer community calls him 'Shroud has 7.6M followers in 2020 on Twitch and up to 200,000 people watched his recent stream-gameplay. These numbers seem to be huge, but in the next 10 years, these will be common among popular streamers.

But let's fold this out. Currently, these stream guys have limited story in their content. Most likely they are talking about the game itself, new patches, daily news, skins and events meanwhile they play the game itself. Why are they still successful? Because they are relatable by the youngsters, the catchy point isn't the gameplay itself, since most of the fans know the game very well. These streamers have the conversation style, which matches perfectly with the 12-25 years old age group. They know how to speak the language of youngsters.

This is one skill that is required for compelling storytelling. I know a lot of non-fiction books, which would be a great hit if it would be told by "a young voice". But it's only one perspective, and we need to see the bigger picture.

Now when we are trying to be creative, we do write our thoughts down. Twitch, Youtube and TikTok are new forms of recording creativity, but not for fiction stories or deeper thoughts. In the upcoming years, we will see a tendency that people will broadcast their **creative stories**—fantasy fictions, cyberpunk stories, maybe thrillers or even non-fiction topics. Live streaming will be the uncut-unedited versions of creative activities, including creating new fiction or non-fiction.

Do you remember when we found out stories in our childhood? The future is the same, just with an adult head. **Creative processes would be more social, and you would be creating (live) content with even the creation process.**

It is a realistic future alternative, where authors tell their ideas, small storylines in live and even the audience could directly interact with these episodes having a direct effect on the outcome. Which means thousands of people literally will "write" one story.

ARTIFICIAL INTELLIGENCE IN BOOK WRITING

In 2020 OpenAI published GPT-3, which was a language model with up to 175 billion ML parameters. One of the capabilities of the application and the model was to heuristically create a certain length of text based on a short input text. But most importantly, the output text was readable for humans. There is a lack of logic in terms of storytelling, but it was at least free of grammatic errors.

What does it mean for us authors?

There would be no need for us in the future?

These were the first questions that emerged in the head of many authors.

Certainly, it isn't the case.

Is it useless?

No, it isn't true; it has a certain level of value even for us authors.

In the following list, I collected the most important use case scenarios of AI technologies. Some of them already exist, but not fully equip the capabilities of Machine

Learning like grammar correction applications, or they are still not 100% like dictation software.

- **Dictation** – The technology exists but dictating, and auto-editing isn't still a mainstream use case for authors, since you can dictate sentence by sentence. This would change in the future when a more flexible approach gets into the action, and authors don't need to pay attention to where they are in the text. Also, it will reduce the after-work drastically.

- **Polishing grammar and readability** – Today's grammar checking tools rely on samples and patterns, but they are limited. AI language models may correct phrases which was never written down. This is a huge opportunity since AI handled text correction happens instantly, which reduces the writing time.

- **Heuristically ending sentences** – Which would also accelerate the writing process. Google is also working on a similar tool, which available in their email client for the English language. These tools could be mainstream in 2-3 years and will be present in every word processing application.

- **Keyword sentences** – We will have the ability to write long sentences using only several keywords or phrases. This tool could essentially help for those who are taking a lot of notes but lack of time to form sentences from them.

There is also an important question concerning using AI for writing. Who will own the intellectual property? The outcome text would be a mix work of the AI and the author. And thanks to language models, the outcome text will be unique and nearly perfect in quality.

Using AI tools for writing could end up that writing style of the authors won't be as important in the future, since AI could easily improve the sentences, or add different writing tone. In other words, this would be a heaven for foreign authors, who don't use English as their mother tongue.

On the other side, the thoughts and ideas behind the lines will be more important—**the story**. Based on my personal experience reading the output lines of GPT-2, it lacks any reasoning. The text doesn't tell you a story, it is more like putting linguistically connected sentences next to each other, but they have no inner meaning.

AI tools will definitely accelerate the writing process in the following 5-10 years when the above functions will be part of the text editors we use on a daily basis.

ARTIFICIAL INTELLIGENCE IN BOOK PUBLISHING

Publishing a book is much easier today than it was ten years ago, but this shift won't end here. Let's see the key elements of preparing a book for publishing:

- Writing the manuscript
- Creating a cover or front creative
- Editing the manuscript
- Proofreading
- Formatting the book
- Narration in case of Audiobooks

Now we can apply future AI tools to these processes hypothetically. We end up that proofreading is the only task where human control is essential. This would be the only fallback option for authors and publishers where if everything goes wrong with AI, human eyes will help in the correction.

Why applying AI is essential for publishers?

It will drastically reduce the costs of the preparation process.

Let's see the average price ranges of the above elements, in case of a 30,000 words book:

- Creating a cover or front creative ($100-500)
- Editing the manuscript ($200-600)
- Proofreading ($100-400)
- Formatting the book ($50-400)
- Narration in case of Audiobooks ($200-500)

I would say well-trained domain-specific AIs may reduce the costs, to almost dollars. Let's see a hypothetic near future (2025-2030) where we utilize AI tools for these purposes (ranges are estimated at today's price level):

- Creating a cover or front creative ($100-400)
- Editing the manuscript ($50-400)
- Proofreading ($10-20)
- Formatting the book ($10-20)
- Narration in case of Audiobooks ($10-20) if we choose non-human narration

I would say only the cover creation and editing will be the two tasks that will be only slightly affected by AI. In the case of these two tasks, AI will only assist humans. In the case of proofreading, formatting and narrating the book will be almost exclusive tasks of the AI programs, and humans will be only controlling points in these processes.

Let's go a little bit further:

The word of publishing will change in the future, and the process won't be the same as today. We will most likely not "writing a story" but "crafting a story".

There could be a time when we just need to decide which formats we intent to release our creative work:

- In written
- In audio
- In motion picture

There will be **auto-publishing services**, where you upload your "crafted mental record" and it will appear on major marketplaces within 5-10 minutes. The quality of these books won't be outstanding but will certainly pass the average quality of today's self-published books overall. The key is here the cost-effectiveness. This would be, in a sense, the "floating glass" of publishing. This will result in a lot of people if not everybody to "write" 2-3 books in his or her lifetime.

But publishing has another important function, to make creative ideas available. This role of the publishing won't change. No matter if it would be a book, an audiobook, or even an *AI animated movie*. But this would be another chapter in this book.

ARTIFICIAL INTELLIGENCE IN BOOK MARKETING

In April 2020, we reached the 1,000th marketing order, which was a milestone for us. We developed a lot of automation solving orders more quickly, like pre-written forms, visual templates, tools that every professional agency utilizes to remain competitive on the market: nothing special, no AI.

The second idea that appeared in us that is it possible to automate a task fully? What if we could train a Machine Learning model to recognize certain patterns.

Let me give you a hypothetic example. We saw up to 1,000 titles in a short period; we check three things in case of every book:

1. **The cover** – Which reflects the quality of the book
2. Amazon Best Seller Rank – In other words, **how successful a book** is
3. **The topic** – Which puts the book into context

We form an inner picture of the book:

- Where is it in its lifecycle?
- Does the price strategy fit to the book?

- Does it have enough recommendation (reviews)?
- Is the genre of the book well defined on the book's page?
- Is the book in a popular genre or a specific niche?

After our picture is complete about the book, we define marketing actions:

Not enough reviews? We need to notify the self-publisher to ask their readers or influencers directly to gain several written feedback or rating.

The Kindle book is overpriced? Explain the partner the right price range for the book preserving its maturity.

The actions are well defined on our side; the answer for a certain situation is more or less the same. Of course, the answer won't be perfect, but it is something that could always be improved.

The fact is that *automation* could check these control points unsupervised in case of any Amazon book. And it may bring 80% of these important actions that should be done on the page. Would you pay $5 for such a quick check? Most likely if it would come back with professional answers and ideas. Which could be provided by the marketing experts in form of pre-written or semi-intelligent options.

Just to give a further idea, pricing a Kindle book has fewer options than you think. It is a finite problem (unless you want to sell books in reality). A Kindle book should be priced somewhere between $1-30. It could be even more expensive, but it will definitely kill sales. Bestseller novels in a length of 300 pages are priced between $10-15 in 2020. We already know the most important price ranges for Kindle books:

- $0.99-2.99 "cheap"
- $3.99-5.99 "average"
- $6.99-9.99 "is it valuable?"
- $10.99-18.99 "best seller wannabe"
- $19.99-29.99 "expensive books"
- $30.99+ "is this a New York Times best seller?"

This is only six price category, and we could easily assign every book into these categories based on the factors described above. For example, a newly released self-published short book should never be in the "best seller wannabe" price category. It would be a complete failure due to only the pricing strategy.

Pricing books automatically

Ok. Now let's imagine this *automatic agent* who could easily analyse the certain parts of the book: title, cover, author's popularity, genre and thanks to machine learning it could assign an appropriate price which would maximize the sale at the actual date and time the book is available. What if this agent could also automatically change the price on KDP? This is the near future. Machine learning or deep learning is capable of handling this problem.

Connecting books and readers with NLP

There is no perfect recommendation system at the moment; even Amazon's AI-powered recommendation system is optimized to maximize **sales**. This resulted in there is a huge gap between bestsellers and ordinary books. The long tail is true today in the book business: 80% of sales are received by 20% of books.

Which isn't good for us readers. We are interested in specific topics, but we haven't the resources and time to find them, only the most popular ones. In the future, Natural Language Processing will be an essential part of recommendation systems. They will analyse the topic of the book, sets, characters-personalities, key events in the book and they will offer the book directly to readers. This approach could end up more books to be visible to readers, and story tips will be ultra-relevant to our tastes.

Automatic story summary

AI will also be able to summarize the story to us readers, along with the above attributes. For example, if we are looking some kick-ass first-contact alien science fiction, it won't be an issue to filter the search results accordingly.

NLP will also be capable of helping the author to list the most important key elements from the book; he or she needs to put into the book description, also in terms of keywords.

AI AND COMPUTER-GENERATED MOVIES ("GEN MOVIES")

One of the most impressing AI subfields is the Generative Adversarial Networks (GANs). These algorithms can process pictures (nature, human faces etc.) from sketch information and put together a detailed output.

How it works? The process is simple, focusing only on the practical side:

- You show thousands of pictures to the model (training set); this way, you teach a neural network to create inner visual abstracts.
- You give input like several hands drawn lines.
- The network-based on its visual abstracts generates a photorealistic

This method also works if you want to draw a person based on his or her voice.

Suppose we scale up the problem from drawing a whole picture from lines to creating a whole movie from a manuscript or book. The necessary steps would be similar to the next figure.

While there are a lot of technical gaps at the moment to build such a system, it is far from impossible:

- There are language models that could extract certain structured data (places, characters, events) from the text.
- With GAN technology we could develop models that could create 3D characters, textures, places, movements, conversations and events from the raw text (at the moment there are no direct efforts towards this but most likely there will be in the coming years)
- We will have a photorealistic 3D engine in the following years (Unreal Engine 5)

We will be able to transform the written text into meaningful visual concepts.

The process is the following in a nutshell:

1. You have a story or manuscript (raw text)
2. A **Language Model** and an **Interpretation Engine** will take apart the text into elements (locations, characters, events and actions)
3. The **3D Environment GAN** will create the locations. Terrains, elements, buildings and the surroundings of the scenes, where the story takes place.

4. The **Actor Model GAN** will generate the plain 3D models of the characters utilizing the details extracted from the text.

5. **Action GAN** will put together a sequence of actions and events into a "structured screenplay" where events could be assigned to certain characters. This requires a so called Action Library, where the system uses pre-defined actions (like jump or walking) that could be applied to the 3D character models.

6. While the story is created live in the 3D engine, and intelligent **Camera AI** is capable to track the actions from the appropriate angles to provide the best experience for the audience.

7. A **Conversation** and a **Music GAN** will produce the sounds based on the **Structured Screenplay**. The conversations could be easily extracted from the Story Manuscript with minor modifications.

8. After the scenes rendered and synchronized with the sound and audio effects, the **"Virtale"** (Virtual Tale) is ready to air

AI AND COMPUTER-GENERATED MOVIES ("GEN MOVIES")

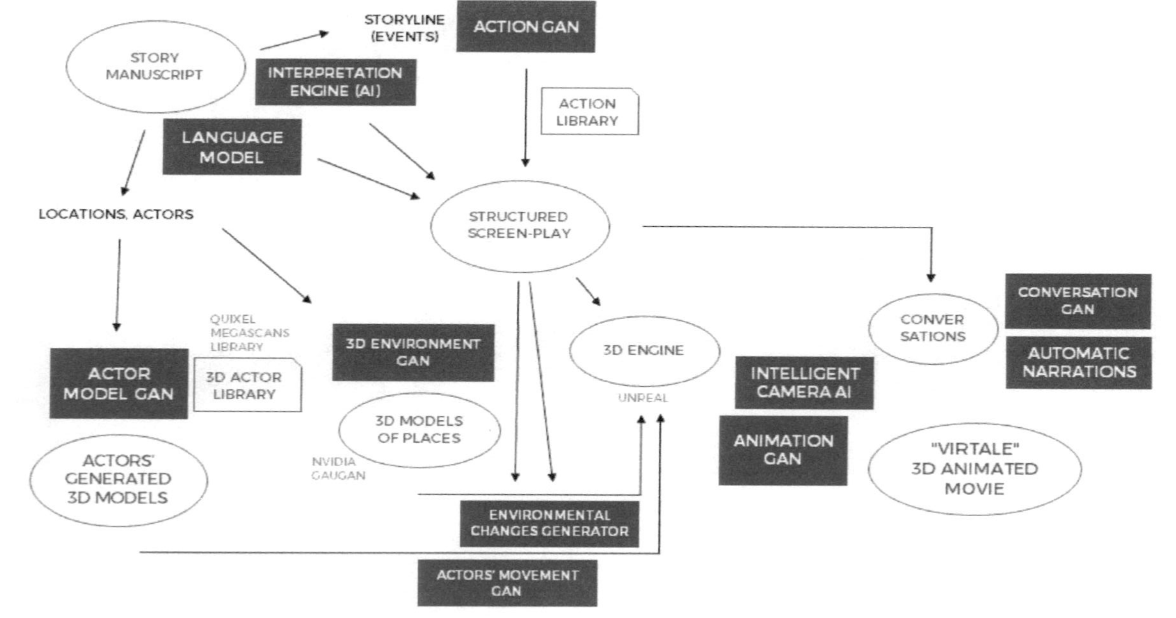

Building up these technologies seems to be science fiction at the moment, but if you are familiar with modern games like The Witcher 3, Last of Us 2, Cyberpunk 2077 they are more like a "movie" than a game. We can call these games as real-time rendered entertainment, where you are the protagonist.

Let me give further utilization of this technology: it could work vice versa. I previously said that younger generations would enjoy the visual story building where they will be part of the story or game. These could be open-world games, **where players will create their own complex** story. And this generative AI engine will also be able to turn it into manuscript or audiobook. Feels crazy.

"You stuck with the story as an author? Just play a little bit in your own generated world and the inspiration will come."

I like this concept, where there will be a direct link between the story and the visual play of the story.

The utilization of GANs will distort the stories, but it won't be more different than putting a book into the screen using the producer's imagination.

SUMMARY

1. **Audiobooks' market will continue to rise** in the next 5-10 years significantly
2. **Production cost and complexity of TV shows and movies will decrease** – Telling a visual story won't be the privilege of Hollywood
3. Live streaming will create new ways how do we publish the stories; the **industry will more rely on creative fictional stories** than now
4. Artificial Intelligence will be an essential part of writing books **helping authors to improve style, grammar and**
5. **AI will be able to handle** several important tasks of the publishing sector, including **editing, proofreading and formatting**. Only creative and controlling parts will remain to professionals.
6. In the future utilizing GANs, interpretation algorithms, and some currently not available AI technologies, we would be able to **turn books into movies**.

"Books are valuable only in hands."

If you enjoyed reading this book or you found some important messages in it, don't hesitate to give it to a friend.

Author's note

This is a self-published book. I choose this form of publication because I deeply believe this is the future. As everything, self-publishing has its drawback at the moment, readers rely more on reviews, so if you could give any feedback to this book on Goodreads or Amazon, it would be a great help for the book.

If you would like to contact the author feel free to email to joel@joelbooks.com

www.ingramcontent.com/pod-product-compliance
Lightning Source LLC
Chambersburg PA
CBHW051126250726
48655CB00007B/2915